GW00862890

EFFECTIVE DISCIPLINE

EFFECTIVE DISCIPLINE

by Jeremy Thorn

The Industrial Society

First published 1977 by
The Industrial Society
Robert Hyde House
48 Bryanston Square
London W1H 7LN
Telephone 071-262 2401

Fourth edition, 1989
© *The Industrial Society, 1977, 1980, 1986, 1989*
Reprinted 1990, 1991

ISBN 0 85290 443 6

British Library Cataloguing in Publication Data
Thorn, Jeremy
    Effective discipline — 4th ed.
    1. Great Britain. Personnel. Discipline. Manuals
    I   Title II.   Series
    658.3'14

Typeset by Senator Graphics, London
Printed and bound in Great Britain by Belmont Press, Northampton

CONTENTS

FOREWORD

Whatever the discipline or level of management, the responsibilities of managers are many and various. It is their job to produce results with essentially just two resources — people and time.

To maximise the potential of both, most managers need some reminders and basic guidelines to help them.

The Notes for Managers series provides succinct yet comprehensive coverage of key management issues and skills. The short time it takes to read each title will pay dividends in terms of utilising one of those key resources — people.

ALISTAIR GRAHAM
Director, The Industrial Society

INTRODUCTION

This booklet sets out to give some basic guidelines which, if adapted to suit each individual situation should make for easier and more productive working relationships. Discipline should not be regarded as either a stick or a carrot with which to coerce the workforce. On the contrary; if discipline is structured in such a way that it is both understood and accepted, it should be evident only by its apparent absence. This will mean that the discipline *is working* and doing the job it is intended to do.

In order to reach and keep such an ultimate degree of good discipline, a great deal of hard work is required: this will, of course, necessitate continual good communication and training.

The remarkable, sometimes obvious, thing about a company running smoothly in the area of discipline, is that, nearly always, all other standards are similarly high. It is often a case of 'you can't have one without the other'. In structuring a code of discipline, many shortcomings may be discovered — and dealt with — which in turn will remove many of the causes of other ancillary problems.

In this age of a more highly educated and informed workforce, just having rules is not good enough; neither is the attitude of simply following minimum legal requirements such as posting statutory requirements on notice boards. Like everything else in life, discipline must have clearly outlined and understood objectives. If discipline is an unstructured, non-objective, and, worse still, misunderstood piece of management legislation, it cannot be expected to work — nor will it.

In this booklet, the basic and practical things on which an effective disciplinary structure can be built will be discussed. The aim is to show discipline as an acceptable, respected, worthwhile and productive aspect of working life.

1

DISCIPLINE

It is probably as well to understand exactly what we mean by the term discipline before delving into the objectives, failures and structures of effective discipline. On consulting a selection of dictionaries we find, in fact, that discipline has quite a range of meanings:

- mental or moral training
- a trained condition
- order maintained, and usually followed by, *a system of rules for conduct* and *a code of acceptable conduct.*

None of the dictionaries consulted, however, described discipline as being punishment. The mistaken view that discipline and punishment are one and the same thing is probably the most usual reason for discipline becoming a distasteful topic. Discipline, in this booklet, will be regarded as either a system of rules for conduct, or a code of acceptable conduct.

Punishment (an unacceptable word nowadays) is better described as *disciplinary action* which will usually result from the breaking or breakdown of the code of conduct. This aspect should not be overlooked as it has a place in the scheme of things. However, the prime objective of discipline is to avoid reaching this stage or, if a breakdown should occur, to recover the situation and re-establish the required conduct. In doing the latter, it should be ensured that all causes or reasons are also assessed and corrective action taken as required.

Finally in this short definition, it is important to understand that there are two basic codes of conduct. They are:

1 accepted disciplines
2 imposed disciplines.

The relationship between these two codes is of prime importance and will be discussed in a later chapter, but basically 'accepted discipline' refers to standards of behaviour, manners, etiquette and courtesy, which may vary slightly according to one's environment but, amazingly, are similar throughout widely spread groups. 'Imposed discipline' refers essentially to rules and regulations, legislation and other statutory requirements.

2

OBJECTIVES

What does discipline set out to achieve? Working in reverse, we will start by summarising the overall objectives of a system of rules. These could be stated as helping to achieve the objectives of:

- the organisation
- the customers
- the employees
- the public and environment
- the future.

Some of these items may well appear to be extraneous to the normal run of discipline matters, so let us develop them a little.

- *The organisation* — could include attendance, work rate, stability, profitability, presentation, public relations, etc.
- *The customer* — service, price, quality, delivery, value, presentation, etc.
- *Employees* — safety, hygiene, welfare, security, wages, etc.
- *Public* — safety (environment), social responsibility, company image.
- *The future* — research effort, long-term security, use of people's creativity, etc.

These are a few of the items which could be considered when setting out to structure a disciplinary code within an organisation. That is not to say that there must be a rule or rules for every aspect as listed, but that the effect of the code of conduct upon these items must be considered.

This is the wider aspect of what discipline sets out to achieve. The approach should be simple. It has been found to be very effective if the workforce is helped to understand the overall objectives and if the workforce knows that success in achieving these objectives affects their future security and prosperity. This is what managing a more informed workforce effectively is all about.

To be effective, a code of discipline (or law) must be seen to be fair, reasonable, logical, and easily understood, and it must be readily acceptable to the majority. To achieve this standard, people must know *why,* as well as *what,* in order to get the correct action.

There are, of course, certain legal minima which must be included in contracts of employment to satisfy such legislation as the Health and Safety at Work Act, the Employment Act and the Employment Protection (Consolidation) Act. The company's rules are drawn up to suit the specific industry, product and environment. These could be listed under the following headings:

- protection and safety — of the person, the company and its resources, products, customers and shareholders
- creation or regulation of codes of behaviour to give parameters within which people can operate to their mutual satisfaction
- outlining minimum standards which will ensure the wellbeing of the company and its employees
- prevention of inefficiency or losses
- presentation of the company as one of good standing in the community.

To achieve all these things, it should not be necessary to publish an enormous volume of rules; it *is* necessary, however, that everyone understands the objectives. This would indicate that good communication, maintained training, and acceptable relationships at all levels are prerequisites to good discipline.

It has already been discovered that legislation without commitment is not the key to better behaviour, but a workforce which is united in achieving its objectives has often proved successful. Be sure before you set out what your objectives really are.

3

EFFECTIVE DISCIPLINE

At this stage it becomes necessary to expand on the two types of discipline normally recognised: the accepted and the imposed.

Infringement

It should be established that there are 'penalties' for infringement of both of these types of discipline. For breaking rules or the law, one may be fined, imprisoned or suffer other forms of punitive action. For breaking accepted codes of behaviour people can be isolated or 'sent to Coventry', all co-operation save the minimum required may be withdrawn or, as once described by one supervisor, they may be 'roasted on the gridiron of public opinion'. These actions may be 'just' according to one's beliefs, but they may not always equate.

Probably the most common breach of the law is to do with road traffic legislation. A person fined heavily for speeding may not be regarded as being guilty of misconduct by his colleagues — indeed he may be given sympathy or regarded as some sort of hero. On the other hand, a blackleg, informant, or someone with really bad manners, though not technically 'guilty', can be brought under such pressure by his colleagues that he is forced to leave the organisation.

Communicating the reason

There are occasions when these two forms of discipline clearly equate. On these occasions, the person will be found 'guilty' by the law and his colleagues. When the accepted and the imposed are both acceptable to the majority, the rule or law is obviously considered reasonable. Thus, to be effective a rule must be considered reasonable by the majority. If it is not, it will probably become an accepted practice to break the rule. When a rule is considered unreasonable, it is not necessarily that it *is* unreasonable; it is almost certainly not understood and often considered to be restrictive.

For example, rules against smoking on an oil refinery are accepted, understood and often policed by the majority. However, rules against smoking in a foundry could be considered to be unreasonable. It may be that there *is* a reason, but unless everyone understands *why* it is almost certain to be ignored and may become the subject of grievance.

Here is an example of an apparently restrictive rule in force over the use of a grinding wheel. A young apprentice was told not to use the grinding wheel for grinding brass and copper laminate. He was not told why and, as he had discovered a way of speeding up his job, thought it was merely the foreman dreaming up restraints. As soon as the foreman's back was turned he used the wheel for this purpose. Shortly after the apprentice finished the job, a fitter used the same grinding wheel to sharpen a large high speed drill. Within seconds, the clogged-up wheel jammed on the drill and disintegrated. The result was the loss of an eye. No punishment could have brought back the eye or made the apprentice any more distraught. Between his sobs he was heard to say: 'If only he had told me why!'

Even if a rule is obvious it *should* be explained: if it is in any way complicated it *must* be explained.

The very best disciplinary rules should be acceptable as well as being imposed. Some would say, if it is acceptable you do not need a rule at all. However, rules are usually for the minority and some framework for conduct is necessary, if only to build standards and procedures on. At the very least, a set of *agreed* procedures should be in existence.

The rule book

When considering the effectiveness of rules, one must consider the rule book. Most organisations have a rule book or set of procedure notes — the latter amount to the same thing but might be considered slightly more democratic. What creates most problems is the needless longevity of some of these rule books. What should be considered to be the lifespan of a rule (or a law)? Obviously (though not actually) a rule should only exist if and when there is a need for it. All too often a rule once made is seldom repealed.

Added to this, there is the annual crop of additions to the rule book. These additions come about due to modern and changing technology and are often very necessary. Recognising that life is fast moving should make it obvious that some rules cease to be necessary and, in fact, may well become restrictive due to their continued existence.

For example, a very large organisation called in a mediator when a large section of the workforce had gone on strike after a worker had been suspended for smoking in a non-smoking area. It should also be stated that a new manager had recently been appointed and had been instructed to tighten up on the seemingly slack discipline. The occurrence had taken place outside in an open space, under a very large NO SMOKING sign. There had been two previous cases and the offenders had been severely warned. At the mediation meeting, attended by the individual, his representatives, the manager and his director, the first question asked by the mediator was: 'Why is that particular place designated a no smoking area?' This was probably the last question expected and no immediate answer was forthcoming. After some debate, the meeting was adjourned with no decision, but with the workers' agreement that they would return to work while enquiries were made.

Some two days later the mediator was telephoned to be told everything was all right; the men were back, all was well. 'Why was it a no smoking area?' After a pause he was told: 'Well, in 1942 we used to store high octane fuel at that spot, so the sign was put up'. 'When did you stop storing it there?' 'Ah — well — in 1944 actually'. So for 30 odd years the sign had been repainted regularly and the reason for its being there had never been queried.

The whole rule book of that organisation was subsequently revised and eventually shrunk to less than a quarter of its original size. The amount of conflict was reduced by considerably more than that amount.

The one-sentence rule for effective discipline is — make it objective, reasonable and easily understood, and involve all those concerned with its structure and maintenance. Finally, avoid those things that will almost certainly be unacceptable and ineffective.

4

RULES AND REGULATIONS

Acceptable rules and regulations (or at least procedure notes) are necessary if only to legislate for that minority who seem incapable of working under an accepted code of behaviour. General objectives and a few of the items to be avoided have already been discussed. It has also been observed that, for the rules to be effective, they must be acceptable, reasonable and clearly understood. Bearing these things in mind, the structuring of rules and regulations will now be discussed.

Creating a structure

Commitment of the workforce to the organisation's objectives is an old established method of getting maximum effort. Involvement and participation have been the 'in' words for a few years now. Therefore, if all levels of the workforce are involved and participate in the structure of a system of rules and regulations, maximum commitment can result, and this will give a good initial start towards acceptance and understanding.

The rules committee should include representatives from both first line management and unions, if they exist; the training department should be involved and the personnel department representative should act as either chairperson or secretary. A similarly structured group should be involved with rules revision.

Types of rules

What rules and regulations are necessary? There are two basic types for any organisation. First, there are the common rules which are those required by law; they include contracts of employment, the Health and Safety at Work Act and its attendant Regulations, industrial relations, and employment protection legislation. Some organisations find it advantageous to publish these separately as they *are* the law, can be amended quite separately, and are not subject to much debate. It should be noted that some of these statutes may vary according to the type of industry: trades such as food and paint spraying have their own specialised regulations which are often difficult to comprehend. They should be carefully interpreted in a simple format. It is essential to find a method of training staff on these, as well as the local requirements.

Secondly, there are organisation rules. The rules committee should have a clear understanding of the objectives these rules are required to meet, before they waste time waffling along on an unknown track. Once they understand clearly what is required, it should not take long to start structuring the basic framework on which they can build required procedures. Normally it takes four or five meetings to define the necessary basics which can be edited to a logical set of notes to establish the rule book.

The most successful rule books are those which state the objective immediately after the individual rule, and also include recommendations for acceptable behaviour which are not necessarily rules. One well-known food company has a rule book comprising only fourteen pages. Seven of these are dedicated to the objectives of the rules — i.e. what is to be achieved. One page is an agreed statement made jointly by unions and management giving their commitment to both rules and objectives. One page outlines disciplinary and appeals procedure and only four contain the rules, leaving a blank page for notes. The book size is only 5" x 3". This has been in use for several years and no problems have yet been encountered.

Brevity

Many lessons can be learned from national legislation — mainly don'ts! *Don't* make excessive rules — think carefully whether five or six separate items can be covered by one good short rule; involve those people covered by the rules or expected to adhere to them. *Don't* try to cover every aspect of interpretation — this usually only leads to more confusion and more loopholes. Brief and clear is the ideal, so the workforce can understand. *Avoid,* like the plague, marginal rules or rules that are only to cover up shortcomings. Above all use commonsense and logic.

Selling the rules

Having got the rules established and written they must be 'sold'. There is absolutely no reason why the committee that was involved in their formation should not also do the training; they can answer any questions which arise and should know the reasons behind each rule. Management and unions together should be involved in implementing and applying rules, as it is advantageous for these influential groups to appear on a platform in accord. The fallout which can thus be obtained is worth all the investment in time. Talking jointly about matters upon which they agree considerably, smooths the path on items upon which they may appear to disagree initially.

If carried out in a calm, logical and well structured manner, formulating a rule book and disciplinary procedures can be a very constructive and worthwhile exercise.

Ensure, however, that the 'forgotten legions' of first line management, i.e. foremen and supervisors, are included at all stages. It will probably be down to them to maintain discipline so their commitment is paramount.

5

DISCIPLINARY ACTION

Having drawn up a set of rules, trained everybody, ensured understanding, and with the best will in the world done all the 'right' things, what happens when a person flagrantly disregards a rule? The time has come to consider disciplinary action. There are many possible actions, all of which appear to be in regular use. Before discussing these, let us first consider what is the underlying objective of any action taken against a proven culprit.

Objectives of action

These seem to cover every aspect of human reaction: punish, set an example, discourage repetition, expose the person — and 'get the person's co-operation and bring him back to an acceptable standard'. This latter case may well sound trite and akin to the psychiatrist's couch but, considered further, it is exactly what is required from any employee — to work to an acceptable standard of performance.

A breach of the disciplinary code means that part of the standard of performance is unacceptable; therefore a return to that standard is the objective. That is not to say that some disciplinary action should not be included, if only to aid memory. However, bearing in mind the ultimate objective, let us consider sanctions in regular use and their effects upon an individual. In this discussion, we are considering the occasional transgressor, not the hardened and regular offender who, failing all attempts to correct, can only be dealt with in one way.

Dismissal

The ultimate sanction — which may well be linked with legal

action in some instances. With current legislation, this is likely to be either the last resort after several warnings, as per procedure, or for one of the well known offences which give no second chance. Examples of these latter offences are smoking on a refinery or in a coal mine, theft, assault, etc. Dismissal should not be taken lightly, nor without first making the fullest enquiries as to the reason for breach of the rule; always ensure a precedent is not being created, or that similar offenders have not been treated differently.

Also make sure that the employee's representative is involved in the procedure if further problems are not to be encountered. Always consider the legal, moral and motivational aspects of dismissal. Dismissal should be very much the last resort.

Suspension

This is still commonly used. In some instances it is illegal if it is without pay, as part of the current legislation spells out that an employer may not remove or reduce an employee's ability to earn as indicated in his terms of employment. If, however, there is an agreement in existence to use suspension as a sanction then suspension can be used. The major factors against suspension without pay are as follows: you may need the person's services; they may leave anyway; they may obtain alternative temporary employment — often at a higher rate; they may well be demotivated enough to withdraw any co-operation and become an irritant to the rest of the workforce. Although in common use, suspension has many side effects that have been given insufficient consideration. Suspension with pay, pending enquiries, or for the individual's well-being or safety (i.e. if incapable of performing duties satisfactorily), is usually understood and acceptable.

Black marks; written warnings

Again, in common use and can be constructive if used correctly. However, if used carelessly, the results of this type of disciplinary action can be extremely poor. Any form of warning *must* be preceded by a full discussion so that the situation is understood.

There must be a prescribed period after which that black mark or warning is withdrawn from the record. If, however, the person understands that the situation can be retrieved by continued good behaviour, it can be a good and constructive form of action. There are exceptions to this last statement, where it may be necessary to keep records. It should also be noted that written warnings should normally follow, in recommended procedure, an informal or non-recorded warning, often described as an informal warning.

Transfer

Once again, a well-worn and common disciplinary action. Usually, it can mean not only a move, but a move to a job of lesser status. The consideration behind a disciplinary transfer is often insufficient. At one end of the scale it can be described as buck passing, at best, it removes a problem from one area only to put a disgruntled employee in another. Even having accepted the transfer with reasonable grace, the person may not be welcomed in the new environment. This can be extremely traumatic and may lead to the individual leaving. If carried out in a constructive manner, and if it allows a square peg to be fitted into a square hole, then the action is not only justified, but constructive to both the individual and the organisation.

Demotion

Can be used right across the organisation, from demoting a foreman back to the bench, to the demotion of a director. The effect upon the individual is about the same. Even when demotion is caused by redundancy, it can hardly be described as a motivator. Quite often, demotion and transfer occur at the same time: this at least allows, on some occasions, a small opportunity to save face. It has often been said that it is kinder to dismiss than demote. The positive side of demotion, like transfer, is when it meets the need of both the individual and the organisation. Instances of this are when people have worked themselves into a position where they cannot cope and may be endangering their health. By common consent, or at least after counselling, there may be a vacancy which the person can fill very satisfactorily. Sideways moves to non-jobs should be avoided. Management also needs to bear in mind claims for constructive dismissal.

Fines

This, like suspension without pay, can be illegal under certain circumstances. Not being paid when late, or cutting a bonus for under-production is a monetary punishment and acceptable. Holding back increments is also acceptable, providing there does not exist a legal agreement to pay. Minimal or no performance review increase is also commonly used and could be described as a fine. All of these, like a black mark, should be retrievable as and when performance improves. However, to be effective, this should be well understood by the person; the period involved should also be known, as should the method of obtaining help if necessary.

Many other possibilities exist and are used.

Interviews

One very important piece of procedure in any disciplinary action is the *discipline* or *grievance interview. All disciplinary action should be preceded by a face-to-face and frank exchange of views.* Even when the individual has been caught red-handed in the most heinous crime, it is important to find out *why;* what was the root cause, the objective, and even the logic (if any) behind the action. The discipline interview can be the single most important action carried out in the whole discipline procedure. To be effective it must be carried out well and structured very carefully.

6

DISCIPLINARY AND GRIEVANCE INTERVIEWS

As has been stated, all disciplinary action should preferably be preceded by an interview to establish the what and why. Of all actions in the cause of good discipline, the well structured and controlled interview can be the most constructive and effective. There are obvious differences between discipline and grievance interviews, but the basic rules remain the same. It should be remembered that, often, the removal of a grievance will avoid having to interview the same employee on the subject of discipline.

Disciplinary interview checklist

Below is a checklist and the method to follow when conducting a disciplinary interview.

1 Purpose

- To inform, and correct, mistakes or bad behaviour, and to prevent this happening again.
- To establish understanding of the standard required and bring the person back to this standard.

2 Preparation

- Gather the facts (consult others, records, rules, procedure, previous record, etc.).
- Do not prejudge issue — guard against bias.
- Plan the approach according to the individual concerned.
- Ensure privacy and no interruptions.
- Allow adequate time.

- Establish the offence.
- Clarify the sanctions available and the authority possessed.
- Notify the time, place and reason for the interview.
- Notify others concerned that the employee will be absent.

3 *Conduct*

- Put the person at ease.
- Establish and advise of offence: be specific.
- Allow the person to state case (listen). This may involve asking open-ended questions (what, when, where, how and who).
- Keep calm (do not argue or use bad language).
- Establish the cause of the problem.
- Be constructive in showing how improvements can take place.
- If possible get interviewee to suggest how improvements can be made.
- Ensure understanding of the standards required.
- State action to be taken by both parties.

4 *Follow up*

- Record the interview (unfair dismissal).
- Check: future behaviour — attitude, performance.
- See necessary help is given if required; check informally with the person concerned to monitor progress.
- Praise and encourage improvements.

Always remember your objective, which is to return the person to an acceptable standard of performance, and ensure the interviewee also understands this objective. Although interviewers must be aware of action available to them, the most vital aspect is getting the interviewee to understand and act to correct their own performance.

Grievance interview checklist

1 *Purpose*

- To enable individuals to air their grievance.
- To discover and remove the cause of dissatisfaction and establish the background.

2 Preparation

- Endeavour to establish circumstances causing dissatisfaction (particularly attitudes, feelings).
- Consult with the people concerned, check previous record/history.
- Be aware of company policy which may affect action which can be taken.
- Ensure privacy and no interruptions.
- Allow adequate time.
- Check that others concerned know where the person will be during the interview.

3 Conduct

- Put the person at ease — establish rapport.
- State the purpose of the interview.
- Allow the individual to state the grievance/problem.
- Get feelings as well as fact — feelings frequently are paramount, facts minimal.
- Listen attentively.
- Do not evade the issue or belittle it.
- Probe in depth to ensure all relevant details are known.
- Investigate facts.
- Do not commit yourself or the organisation too quickly.
- If possible, get the individual to suggest solutions.
- State proposed course of action — if known at this stage. If no decision has been reached, then state the nature of future action.

4 Follow up

- Investigate the facts/information if necessary.
- Decide on the action in light of investigation, and communicate to the person concerned.
- Check that results are as required — relationships, attitudes, performance.
- Record only if necessary.
- Make sure the person is seen informally later, if only for a few seconds.

Points to consider

During discipline interviews, the employee's representative is entitled to be present. However, it is often more constructive to carry out the initial interview on a one-to-one basis. Employees should be clearly told that if at any time they may wish to have their representative present, they can do so, but until that time a better understanding may be established on a face-to-face basis. Should a worker's representative be present, the interviewer would be well advised also to have a back-up.

The grievance interview can often prove constructive by just listening. Care should be taken, however, not to allow too much time to the organisation's 'professional moaner', nor to react to non-established problems. The grievance interview, however, can often be an early warning system.

People have often queried the approaches in setting up discipline interviews. To get the best results, adopt an informal attitude, certainly at first/verbal warning stage. The atmosphere may need to become formal if the disciplinary action has to continue to formal/final warning stages. A discipline interview is not different to any other. If both parties are on tenterhooks and wish to get the thing over, nothing useful will result. On the other hand, careful and considerate handling pays dividends. For example, one well known organisation discovered unused talent and established an exceedingly useful member of staff (now the works manager). His words at a discipline interview were: 'That's the first time anybody has ever listened and agreed to help'. The lesson learned was that if a person's creativity and talent are not fully harnessed for the use of the organisation, it may still be used — against the organisation.

7

CAUSES OF BREACHES
OF DISCIPLINE

It is probably true to say that there are a million causes for breaches of discipline, all with different accents. However, an analysis of a fairly large selection of these breaches established only three root causes, as follows:

- for gain — 20% (including all aspects of 'gain')
- due to frustration — 75%
- other — 5% (miscellaneous events).

Of the organisations surveyed, it was found that in any one year, 4 per cent or less of the employees were involved with action under the heading of 'disciplinary'. As approximately 75 per cent of these occurrences were due to frustration, some further study was made to establish the events leading up to this frustration. In most cases it followed a definable pattern: starting with some kind of misunderstanding, each event in the series had a reaction which in turn resulted in undesirable side effects. The route is normally as follows:

- *misunderstanding* followed by
- *simple problem* or *complaint* which, if not dealt with, leads to *resentment*
- *actual grievance* which, if not dealt with, leads to *aggression* or *regression*
- *dissatisfaction* which, if not dealt with, leads to *depression*
- *frustration* and *fixation* which, if not dealt with, lead to *apathy*.

It was found that a majority of the people with queries were not discussing them with their bosses, and often, after discussion with their colleagues, the wrong answer was found. If the problem was large enough to make it imperative to ask the boss, various types of reaction resulted.

Q 'Have you got a minute?'
A 'Does it have to be now? I'm very busy.'
   'See the wages people, it's their problem.'
   'Personnel can sort that out.'
   'That's not your problem.'

These and many other similar answers, all lead into grievance and a 'couldn't care less' attitude. They are also signs of either an irresponsible or an overworked boss. In any event, one must always remember that, to individuals, their 'minor' complaint is of the greatest importance. It must be dealt with as quickly as possible — often just listening to the problem significantly reduces its effect. Unresolved problems will lead either to labour turnover or discipline situations.

One complaint often voiced by first line managers is that their authority has been reduced to virtually zero. It may be that they give their authority away by directing all their problems to senior or specialist management. Here, the case for a set procedure being adhered to is paramount. All problems must first be dealt with by the immediate boss and must only be passed on if they are insoluble at that level.

Managers should:

Diagnose

As a general rule, humans are not instinctive animals, but experienced and knowledgeable managers will develop a sixth sense which will warn of any impending crisis. These managers make a study of the individuals under their control and probably will have developed a good relationship with the workers' representative. Thus, successful managers will find time to walk the job and will not allow pressures to bog them down in the office. They will also be good delegators, successful motivators and, probably, well liked by the workforce. All of this will amount to a happy and effective workforce where disciplinary problems are less likely to occur.

Anticipate problems

No amount of rules, regulations or procedures can substitute for the application of commonsense. With the pressures of modern working life, the urgent often takes priority over the important, which leads eventually to the important cropping up as urgent when it gets out of control. Systematic priorities and good anticipation, together with the ability to shed the streams of excess information, all help to make the best use of time and avoid crises. Most important in the field of discipline is the encouragement of people and their representatives to discuss problems in the embryonic stage: to get maximum effectiveness from this one must always be prepared to listen and act. As ever, prevention is by far the most effective cure.

8

JOB DESCRIPTION — STANDARDS OF PERFORMANCE

What do job descriptions and standards of performance have to do with discipline? In essence everything, especially when dealing with individuals, and it is usually to individuals that we apply codes of conduct. Seldom do we find that a discipline problem is connected with an entire group, unless we are dealing with organised crime — which is outside the confines of this book.

Understanding what is required of a person at work is almost the first step in establishing a good code of conduct. The contract of employment should deal with the legal requirements and outline the basis of hours, holidays, attendance and sickness. This is not a job description, but the basic requirements of an employee. All employees should have and understand their job description which should be in two parts.

1 A basic description of the job and its activities — not in great detail which only leads to 'who does what' arguments — but in generalities outlining objectives to be achieved.
2 A set of ongoing standards which must be continually achieved to be able to say an acceptable standard is being maintained.

Drawing up a job description

The total of these two parts of a job description should not cover more than two pages. All items included should contribute to the overall objectives of the organisation. Part one must include:

- to whom the employee is directly responsible (the boss — one only)
- for whom the employee is responsible (subordinates — numbers and names)
- lines of communication or liaison on a regular basis
- job title and objectives (in general terms) of the operation
- limits of authority under headings such as finance, people, communication, product or material, etc.
- training and development of subordinates
- any other items relevant to a particular job or profession.

A question often asked is: 'Who should write the job descriptions?' The simple answer is the job holders themselves. That is to say, the original draft should be drawn up by the job holder, then discussed, amended and *agreed* with the boss. This gives an ideal opportunity to get a mutual understanding towards the objectives and aims of the organisation and the job holders' contributions. It also allows the bosses to rationalise the jobs of their subordinates. Copies should be held by the job holders, their bosses and the personnel department. It should be noted that the job holder *agrees* and *understands* what is required by the job description.

Part two should be the standards of acceptable performance. Every job holder should have, and understand, a set of ongoing standards of performance, and each standard should be related to part one of the job description. Basic rules must be given when drawing up standards *with* the job holder.

1 Each standard should be preceded with the phrase, 'I will have attained an acceptable standard when . . . .'
2 Every standard must be *realistic* not *idealistic;* that is to say, it must be achievable, not a dream.
3 Every standard should leave room for improvement — for instance, on an occasional and short-term basis when a sprint is required to cover an emergency situation.
4 Every standard must be quantifiable or measurable using standards like time, percentages, number of other measures.
5 All must be agreed and not forced. If force is required, there will be another problem to solve.

Advantages

The advantages of having standards of performance on an ongoing basis are many. The first is that job holders have an early opportunity of understanding what is expected of them. The discussion to agree these standards allows for many queries to be raised and solved.

One of the greatest advantages for having standards of performance is that, during times of appraisal, bosses have measurable standards by which to appraise, thus removing all temptation to appraise subjectively. During the appraisal, one can identify areas of weakness in the job and apply corrective action in the form of training. Appraisals carried out in this way, with the job holder being able to see help coming from the appraisal, are more likely to be acceptable and ensure co-operation. It also means that, in an interview situation, the interviewer can discuss performance against facts.

When all else fails, any question of wrongful dismissal is removed, as the job holder knew what was required in quantifiable terms. The total knowledge of the job and what is involved sets a good foundation for an effective code of conduct.

9

LEADERSHIP AND DISCIPLINE

One way by which to raise the morale, and therefore the standard of behaviour of people at work, is by good and effective leadership, which must include the involvement of the work-group and the individuals in that group.

Effective leadership in itself will create within the team a supportive atmosphere, which means that a self-discipline is created and the team will tend to monitor its own standards. Part of an individual's task as leader is to ensure that communication is good and that their workers thoroughly understand the objectives and their necessary contribution towards the achievement of these objectives. Further still, by involving the team and individuals in distribution of tasks, the leader can get a high level of commitment from the people, which again will contribute to good discipline and high performance.

An effective leader will almost certainly give and receive respect to and from the team. Workers with high regard for their leaders are much less likely to carry out acts against the organisation than people who work in an environment where the work-group leader merely dishes out work and discipline. It has often been observed that, where the work-group is of a reasonable size which the leader can manage, and where the leader has the authority to carry out the total leadership role, the incidence of breaches of discipline is low.

A good leader is an accepted leader and will always endeavour to help, advise and listen to team members. Individuals will get reassurance and the leader will show enthusiasm for their ideas. In such circumstances it is rare for people to rock the boat. In return, the team will support the leader and output will be high. Good leadership is almost a prerequisite to good discipline, since a bad leader will often be rewarded by a troubled discipline scene.

10

INDUCTION AND TRAINING FOR DISCIPLINE

New employees, whether in their first job or their umpteenth, have three basic worries: will I be able to cope; will they like me; will I fit in? Starting any new job is a traumatic period in anybody's life and, when one is concerned with such questions, it is not a good time to try to assimilate any heavy, and maybe incomprehensible, lists of rules, regulations, do's and dont's.

First-day induction on discipline procedures should only include those things which are a must. These, of course, must include items to do with safety, and the obvious necessity of where and when to report and to whom the new employee is responsible.

Once the first week is over and the new starters are more settled, it is time to give the kind of input which requires some attention, and to give an outline of the organisation. The object here, however, is not induction, but discipline.

Sometimes newcomers are issued on their arrival with sets of books and manuals, including the rule book, and are told to read them. It is doubtful whether more than 1 per cent ever do, and if they do it is even more doubtful whether they understand the rules or the reasons for them. After a short period of working, the chances of understanding are increased, but then it is even more important to have the rules explained so that the reasons for them can be discussed and any questions answered. Most rule books are structured so that over half of them are common to all organisations. Some of these common rules are also law and therefore are unnecessary in a rule book, merely serving to bulk it. It is no sin to have a 'small' rule book.

With regard to discipline, the obvious person to discuss this is the starter's boss who will be the individual responsible for his conduct. By allowing the boss to do this job, authority begins to be established and the employee begins to respond to the boss. Their initial response to each other if this is carried out sympathetically, will initiate an early understanding and willingness to co-operate.

Induction is very important in establishing a code of conduct and may well establish a trend which can obviate future problems (see *Induction,* in this series).

11

SUMMARY

As in all things, a practical, honest, and simple approach offers the best return in matters of discipline. Additionally, good management will pay dividends in the field of discipline. Foremost are the following.

- Does everybody know and understand what the disciplinary code sets out to achieve?
- Have all levels been consulted in setting up the procedures?
- Does the procedure set time limits and is it geared for swift solving of grievances/problems?
- Have all the managers had a basic grounding in leadership techniques? Good leadership is paramount to good discipline.
- Have unions, if they exist, been fully involved and are they instructively committed to a good standard of behaviour?

Attention is required at all times to ensure continual good discipline because, like most things, maintenance and the ability to spot latent problems are essential. Understanding is a key which opens many doors and, as soon as mutual respect is established, so too are the roots of a good disciplinary atmosphere.

Legislation

Employment legislation is not a new phenomenon in this country, although it has become of greater importance in the late 1980s.

In any disciplinary situation it is important to know what obligations and restrictions the law places on a manager as well as to be aware of the correct procedure. This is particularly so of dismissal.

It has become the practice in recent years for one new piece of legislation to amend or repeal part of existing statute law and it is, therefore, vital that where there is any doubt on an area affected by legislation, you seek advice. The most fruitful sources of advice will be your own organisation's personnel department, the Department of Employment, the Information Department of The Industrial Society, or the Society's relevant publications.

The subject of employment practices and law are dealt with thoroughly in *A guide to employment practices,* in this series, and *A guide to the employment acts,* by Joan Henderson, also published by The Industrial Society.

APPENDICES

APPENDIX 1

EFFECTIVE DISCIPLINE CHECKLIST

1 Has a disciplinary code been drawn up in consultation with all levels of the workforce?

2 Are the rules and regulations reviewed annually to keep them in line with the needs of the organisation and limited to a minimum of items?

3 Does a disciplinary procedure exist and is it adhered to logically?

4 Does a system exist whereby *all* employees not only have copies of rules and procedures, but have been trained in their use and thoroughly understand them and their objectives?

5 If there are unions, have they been consulted from the outset; do they understand their part?

6 Is a fair and understood management development plan working in the organisation to enable all employees to benefit from the training and possible promotion?

7 Does a structured appraisal system exist, linked closely to agreed standards of performance?

8 Do all those in charge of others receive basic training on all aspects of discipline, grievance, and work-group maintenance?

9 Does the workforce agree all the concepts upon which the disciplinary code is based? Does the disciplinary code concur with socially desirable items?

10 Is there an appeals procedure that enables those people being disciplined to have every opportunity to put forward all aspects of their case?

11 Is the code accepted as an integral part of the management–union agreement?

APPENDIX 2

DISCIPLINARY CODE

'Disciplinary rules and procedures are necessary for promoting fairness and order in the treatment of individuals and in the conduct of industrial relations. They also assist an organisation to operate effectively. Rules set standards of conduct at work; procedure helps to ensure that the standards are adhered to and also provides a fair method of dealing with alleged failures to observe them.'

Main provisions

1 Define rules in writing and set standards. Define penalties for serious offences — preferably after discussion with trade union. Make rules known to each employee. Avoid unnecessary rules — review all rules and use of discipline procedure at least every two years.

2 Establish whether there has been an offence and what the circumstances are before deciding appropriate action. What are the facts? Does the behaviour make sense? What is the reason/underlying cause?

3 Ensure individuals understand the standard required. Confront them with their failure and aim to get them to change their ways — first by informal and then by formal warning, indicating the consequences of continued failure to meet the standards.

4 Provide evidence of previous warning/behaviour by a written record/warning. Basic justice requires that the disciplinary action can be subtantiated to an 'outsider'.

5 Refer case to someone not directly involved before enforcing sanctions (personnel/establishment officer or more senior manager).

6 Provide means of objection/appeal.

7 Specify limits of authority for supervisors/managers.

Essential features of a disciplinary procedure

It should:

- be in writing
- specify to whom it applies
- provide for matters to be dealt with quickly
- indicate the disciplinary actions which may be taken
- specify the levels of management which have the authority to take the various forms of disciplinary action, ensuring that immediate supervisors do not normally have the power to dismiss without reference to senior management
- provide for individuals to be informed of the complaints against them and to be given an opportunity to state their case before decisions are reached
- give individuals the right to be accompanied by a union representative or by a fellow employee of their choice
- ensure that, except for gross misconduct, no employees are dismissed for a first breach of discipline
- ensure that disciplinary action is not taken until the case has been carefully investigated
- ensure that individuals are given an explanation for any penalty imposed
- provide a right of appeal and specify the procedure to be followed.

When operating disciplinary procedure, management should view the prime objective as encouraging improvements in the employee, rather than the imposition of sanctions. Action must be taken promptly as delay allows facts and recollections to fade, and could be interpreted by individuals as management condoning their actions. Only in serious cases should consideration be given to suspension (with pay) for a limited period to establish facts.

In the main, the first formal step ought to be a formal oral warning, followed by a written warning, followed by a final written warning, followed by discharge. However, the type of warning issued will depend on the magnitude of the offence. Records are important not only for evidence before a tribunal, but as an indication of what has happened in order that all involved parties are in no doubt as to what the offence was and what corrective action is needed.

FURTHER READING

The human side of enterprise, by Douglas McGregor, London: McGraw Hill.

Training for leadership, Dr John Adair, London: Gower, 1978.

Effective leadership, Dr John Adair, London: Gower.

Work and the nature of man, Frederick Herzberg, Cleveland: World Publishing, 1966.

Motivation and personality, A. H. Maslow, New York: Harper and Row, 1970.

Up the organisation, Robert Townsend, London: Michael Joseph.

The manager's guide to the behavioural sciences, Margaret Brown, The Industrial Society.

A guide to employment practices. Notes for Managers. Betty Ream, London: *The Industrial Society, 1989.*

A guide to the employment acts, Joan Henderson, The Industrial Society, 1988.